A Brush with Burns

A Brush with Burns

Poems by Robert Burns

Illustrated by

Elizabeth Blackadder

Introduction by Ian Campbell

Collected and edited by Lucina Prestige

Renaissance Press

First Published 2014
Renaissance Press
Edinburgh

Illustrations © Elizabeth Blackadder

ISBN 9780 954 396152

Printed by Multiprint, Kirkcaldy, Scotland

Introduction

Fareweel, my rhyme-composing billie!
Your native soil was right ill-willie;
But may ye flourish like a lily,
Now bonilie!
I'll toast you in my hindmost gillie,
Tho owre the sea!

Except, of course, that Burns did not head overseas in 1786, but stayed in Scotland to add to his marvellous output. *On a Scotch Bard* hits his position on the head when it pinpoints the lack of profit Burns made from Scotland in his lifetime: but it underlines too his complete commitment to the country, and his ironic sense of the difference between the lily he might become in sunny Jamaica, and the thrawn hard-drinking plant he saw himself in his own country. Burns was no lily, surely. But the poems which follow highlight again and again his sensitivity to the birds, the flowers, the animals of his native country.

Obviously, Burns found time in a lifetime of achingly hard work, unrelenting sociability, song collecting, family life, and tossing back his hindmost gillies to mark the countryside with which he is universally associated. Sometimes he stops to give serious consideration in close-up – the mouse scuttling away from the wrecked nest in the ploughed field, the louse observed in a minute's boredom during service crawling up a lady's clothes. More often, in these poems, he takes a wider view, the birds singing, the animals in all the seasons, the countryside which after all formed the backdrop to most of his adult and working life. The references to nature may be merely in passing, or they may (in the case of the red rose) be the image round which the whole song, as shaped and re-shaped by Burns with his wonderful economy of image, revolves: the exaggeration of the seas running dry and the melting rocks does nothing to detract from the sensuously appropriate image, the flower freshly bloomed, its scent intact, a perfectly judged link to the poem's other images of beauty and natural perfection.

Burns' reflection of nature is all the more astonishing when we consider how much of it he must have experienced in the close-up of rain and wind and hours of back-breaking labour. But these verses show that he could reach into the catalogue of bird and beast and natural phenomenon in song, in serious poetry, in his skilful adaptation of collected poems from other sources: his skill in matching words to melody has been much noted, but he has skill too in finding the right image from nature to reinforce his effect.

These poems rescue Burns from the painful statues which show him pensively holding an uprooted daisy. For Burns' nature was inescapably alive, various, colourful, and Elizabeth Blackadder's brush brings that pulsing energy vividly to life. "There's nae life like the ploughman's in the month o sweet May", he wrote. The proof is here.

Ian Campbell

Acknowledgements

Ian Campbell, David and Barbara Bruce and Eddie Ross for all their help in making this book.

INDEX

By Allan Stream

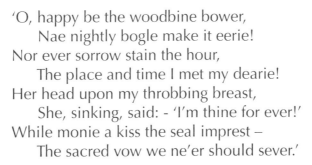

By Allan stream I chanc'd to rove,
    While Phoebus sank beyond Benledi;
The winds were whispering thro the grove,
    The yellow corn was waving ready;
I listen'd to a lover's sang,
    An thought on youthfu pleasures monie,
And ay the wild-wood echoes rang: -
    'O, my love Annie's very bonie!'

'O, happy be the woodbine bower,
    Nae nightly bogle make it eerie!
Nor ever sorrow stain the hour,
    The place and time I met my dearie!
Her head upon my throbbing breast,
    She, sinking, said: - 'I'm thine for ever!'
While monie a kiss the seal imprest –
    The sacred vow we ne'er should sever.'

The haunt o Spring's the primrose-brae.
    The Summer joys the flocks to follow.
How cheery thro her short'ning day
    Is Autumn in her weeds o yellow!
But can they melt the glowing heart,
    Or chain the soul in speechless pleasure,
Or thro each nerve the rapture dart,
    Like meeting her, our bosom's treasure?

To a Mountain Daisy
On turning one down with the plough, in April 1786

Wee, modest, crimson-tippèd flow'r,
Thou's met me in an evil hour;
For I maun crush amang the stoure
    Thy slender stem:
To spare thee now is past my pow'r.
    Thou bonie gem.

Alas! it's no thy neebor sweet,
The bonie lark companion meet,
Bending thee 'mang the dewy weet,
    Wi spreckl'd breast!
When upward-springing, blythe, to greet
    The purpling east.

Cauld blew the bitter-biting north
Upon thy early, humble birth;
Yet cheerfully thou glinted forth
    Amid the storm,
Scarce rear'd above the parent-earth
    Thy tender form.

The flaunting flow'rs our gardens yield,
High shelt'ring woods and wa's maun shield;
But thou, beneath the random bield
      O clod or stane,
Adorns the histie stibble-field,
      Unseen, alane.

There, in thy scanty mantle clad,
Thy snawie bosom sun-ward spread,
Thou lifts thy unassuming head
      In humble guise;
But now the share uptears thy bed,
      And low thou lies!

Such is the fate of artless maid,
Sweet flow'ret of the rural shade!
By love's simplicity betray'd,
      And guiless trust;
Till she, like thee, all soil'd, is laid
      Low i' the dust.

Such is the fate of simple Bard,
On Life's rough ocean luckless starr'd!
Unskilful he to note the card
    Of prudent lore,
Till billows rage, and gales blow hard,
    And whelm him o'er!

Such fate to suffering Worth is giv'n,
Who long with wants and woes has striv'n,
By human pride or cunning driv'n
    To mis'ry's brink;
Till, wrench'd of ev'ry stay but Heav'n,
    He, ruin'd, sink!

Ev'n thou who mourn'st the Daisy's fate,
That fate is thine – no distant date;
Stern Ruin's plough-share drives elate,
    Full on thy bloom,
Till crush'd beneath the furrow's weight,
    Shall be thy doom!

Ay Waukin, O

Ay waukin, O,
    Waukin still and weary:
Sleep I can get nane
    For thinking on my dearie.

Simmer's a pleasant time;
    Flowers of every colour,
The water rins owre the heugh,
    And I long for my true lover.

When I sleep I dream,
    When I wauk I'm eerie,
Sleep I can get nane,
    For thinking on my dearie.

Lanely night comes on,
    A' the lave are sleepin,
I think on my bonie lad,
    And I bleer my een wi greetin.

Beware o Bonie Ann

Ye gallants bright, I rede you right,
    Beware o bonie Ann!
Her comely face sae fu o grace,
    Your heart she will trepan:
Her een sae bright, like stars by night,
    Her skin is like the swan.
Sae jimply lac'd, her genty waist,
    That sweetly ye might span.

Youth, Grace, and Love attendant move,
    And Pleasure leads the van:
In a' their charms, and conquering arms,
    They wait on bonie Ann.
The captive bands may chain the hands
    But Love enslaves the man:
Ye gallants braw, I rede you a',
    Beware o bonie Ann!

SWAN.

From **Address to the Deil**

When thowes dissolve the snawy hoord,
An float the jinglin icy boord,
Then, water-kelpies haunt the foord,
    By your direction,
An 'nighted trav'llers are allur'd
    To their destruction.

On Sensibility

Sensibility how charming,
    Thou, my friend, canst truly tell!
But Distress with horrors arming
    Thou alas! hast known too well!

Fairest flower, behold the lily
    Blooming in the sunny ray:
Let the blast sweep o'er the valley,
    See it prostrate in the clay.

Hear the woodlark charm the forest,
    Telling o'er his little joys;
But alas! a prey the surest
    To each pirate of the skies!

Dearly bought the hidden treasure
    Finer feelings can bestow:
Chords that vibrate sweetest pleasure
    Thrill the deepest notes of woe.

Behold, my Love, how Green the Groves

Behold, my love, how green the groves,
    The primrose banks how fair;
The balmy gales awake the flowers,
    And wave thy flowing hair.

The lav'rock shuns the palace gay,
    And o'er the cottage sings:
For Nature smiles as sweet, I ween,
    To Shepherds as to Kings.

Let minstrels sweep the skilfu strings,
    In lordly lighted ha':
The Shepherd stops his simple reed,
    Blythe in the birken shaw.

The Princely revel may survey
    Our rustic dance wi scorn;
But are their hearts as light as ours,
    Beneath the milk-white thorn?

The shepherd, in the flowery glen;
    In shepherd's phrase, will woo:
The courtier tells a finer tale,
    But is his heart as true?

These wild-wood flowers I've pu'd, to deck
　　That spotless breast o thine:
The courtier's gems may witness love,
　　But, 'tis nae love like mine.

Sleep'st Thou

Sleep'st thou, or wauk'st thou, fairest creature?
    Rosy Morn now lifts his eye,
Numbering ilka bud, which Nature
    Waters wi the tears o joy.
    Now to the streaming fountain
    Or up the healthy mountain
The hart, hind, and roe, freely, wildly-wanton stray;
    In twining hazel bowers,
    His lay the linnet pours,
    The laverock to the sky
    Ascends, wi sangs o joy.
While the sun and thou arise to bless the day!

Phoebus, gilding the brow of morning,
    Banishes ilk darksome shade,
Nature, gladdening and adorning:
    Such to me my lovely maid!
    When frae my Chloris parted,
    Sad, cheerless, broken-hearted,
The night's gloomy shades, cloudy, dark, o'ercast my sky;
    But when she charms my sight
    In pride of Beauty's light,
    When thro my very heart
    Her beaming glories dart,
'Tis then – 'tis then I wake to life and joy!

Will ye go to the Indies, My Mary

Will ye go to the Indies, my Mary,
    And leave auld Scotia's shore?
Will ye go to the Indies, my Mary,
    Across th' Atlantic's roar?

O, sweet grows the lime and the orange,
    And the apple on the pine;
But a' the charms o the Indies
    Can never equal thine.

I hae sworn by the Heavens to my Mary,
    I hae sworn by the Heavens to be true,
And sae may the Heavens forget me,
    When I forget my vow!

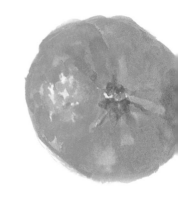

O, plight me your faith, my Mary,
    And plight me your lily-white hand!
O, plight me your faith, my Mary,
    Before I leave Scotia's strand!

We hae plighted our troth, my Mary,
    In mutual affection to join;
And curst be the cause that shall part us!
    The hour and the moment o time!

From **Tam Lin**

She had na pu'd a double rose,
    A rose but only tway,
Till up then started young Tom-lin
    Says, Lady, thou's pu nae mae.

Janet has kilted her green kirtle
    A little aboon her knee,
And she has snooded her yellow hair,
    A little aboon her bree,
And she is to her father's ha,
    As fast as she can hie.

From **Address to the Deil**

When wi an eldritch, stoor 'quaick, quaick.'
    Amang the springs,
Awa ye squatter'd like a drake,
    On whistling wings.

Epitaph on Holy Willie

Here Holy Willie's sair worn clay
    Taks up its last abode;
His saul has ta'en some other way -
    I fear, the left-hand road.

Stop! there he is as sure's a gun!
    Poor, silly body, see him!
Nae wonder he's as black's the grun -
    Observe wha's standing wi him!

Your brunstane Devilship, I see
    Has got him there before ye!
But haud your nine-tail cat a wee,
    Till ance you've heard my story.

Your pity I will not implore,
    For pity ye have nane.
Justice, alas! has gi'en him o'er,
    And mercy's day is gane.

But hear me, Sir, Deil as ye are,
    Look something to your credit:
A cuif like him wad stain your name,
    If it were kent ye did it!

To a Mouse
On Turning up her nest with the Plough
November 1785

Wee sleekit, cow'rin, tim'rous beastie,
O, what a panic's in thy breastie!
Thou need na start awa sae hasty,
    Wi bickering brattle!
I wad be laith to rin an chase thee,
    Wi murdering pattle!

I'm truly sorry man's dominion
Has broken Nature's social union,
An justifies that ill opinion,
    Which makes thee startle
At me, thy poor, earth-born companion,
    An fellow mortal!

I doubt na, whyles, but thou may thieve;
What then? poor beastie, thou maun live!
A daimen icker in a thrave
    'S a sma request;
I'll get a blessin wi the lave,
    An never miss't!

Thy wee-bit housie, too, in ruin!
Its silly wa's the win's are strewin!
An naething, now, to big a new ane,

O foggage green!
An bleak December's win's ensuin,
     Baith snell an keen!

Thou saw the fields laid bare an waste,
An weary winter comin fast,
An cozie here, beneath the blast,
     Thou thought to dwell,
Till crash! the cruel coulter past
     Out thro thy cell.

That wee bit heap o leaves an stibble,
Has cost thee monie a weary nibble!
Now thou's turn'd out, for a' thy trouble,
     But house or hald,
To thole the winter's sleety dribble,
     An cranreuch cauld!

But Mousie, thou art no thy lane,
In proving foresight may be vain:
The best-laid schemes o mice and men
     Gang aft agley,
An lea'e us nought but grief an pain,
     For promis'd joy!

Still thou art blest, compar'd wi me!
The present only toucheth thee:
But och! I backward cast my e'e,
    On prospects drear!
An forward, tho I canna see,
    I guess an fear!

From **Death and Doctor Hornbook.**

The rising moon began to glow'r
The distant Cumnock Hills out-owre:
To count her horns, wi a' my pow'r,
    I set mysel:
But whether she had three or four,
    I cou'd na tell.

Helleborus

O, Bonie Was Yon Rosy Brier

O, bonie was yon rosy brier
    That blooms sae far frae haunt o man,
And bonie she – and ah, how dear! –
    It shaded frae the e'enin sun!

Yon rosebuds in the morning dew,
    How pure among the leaves sae green!
But purer was the lover's vow
    They witness'd in their shade yestreen.

All in its rude and prickly bower,
    That crimson rose how sweet and fair!
But love is far a sweeter flower
    Amid life's thorny path o care.

The pathless wild and wimpling burn,
    Wi Chloris in my arms, be mine,
And I the warld nor wish nor scorn –
    Its joy and griefs alike resign!

My Hoggie

What will I do gin my hoggie die?
　　My joy, my pride, my hoggie!
My only beast, I had nae mae,
　　And vow but I was vogie!
The lee-lang night we watched the fauld,
　　Me and my faithfu doggie;
We heard nocht but the roaring linn,
　　Among the braes sae scroggie.

But the houlet cry'd frae the castle wa',
　　The blitter frae the boggie,
The tod reply'd upon the hill:
　　I trembled for my hoggie.
When day did daw, and cocks did craw,
　　The morning it was foggie,
An unco tyke lap o'er the dyke,
　　And maist has kill'd my hoggie!

The Night was Still

The night was still, and o'er the hill
    The moon shone on the castle wa',
The mavis sang, while dew-drops hang
    Around her on the castle wa':

Sae merrily they danc'd the ring
    Frae eenin till the cock did craw,
And ay the o'erword o the spring
    Was: 'Irvine's bairns are bonie a'!'

From **Tam O Shanter**

But pleasures are like poppies spread:
You seize the flow'r, its bloom is shed;
Or like the snow falls in the river,
A moment white – then melts for ever;
Or like the borealis race,
That flit ere you can point their place;
Or like the rainbow's lovely form
Evanishing amid the storm.
Nae man can tether time or tide,
The hour approaches Tam maun ride:
That hour o night's black arch the key-stane,
That dreary hour Tam mounts his beast in:
And sic a night he taks the road in,
As ne'er poor sinner was abroad in.

The Birks of Aberfeldie

Chorus
Bonie lassie, will ye go,
Will ye go, will ye go?
Bonie lassie, will ye go,
    To the birks of Aberfeldie?

Now simmer blinks on flow'ry braes,
And o'er the crystal streamlets plays,
Come, let us spend the lightsome days
    In the birks of Aberfeldie!

The little birdies blythely sing,
While o'er their heads the hazels hing,
Or lightly flit on wanton wing
    In the birks of Aberfeldie!

The braes ascend like lofty wa's,
The foaming stream, deep roaring, fa's
O'erhung wi fragrant-spreading shaws
    The birks of Aberfeldie.

The hoary cliffs are crown'd wi flowers,
White o'er the linns the burnie pours,
And rising, weets wi misty showers
    The birks of Aberfeldie.

Let Fortune's gifts at random flee,
They ne'er shall draw a wish frae me,
Supremely blest wi love and thee
    In the birks of Aberfeldie.

Of A' the Airts
The Wind can Blaw

Of a' the airts the wind can blaw
    I dearly like the west,
For there the bonie lassie lives,
    The lassie I lo'e best.
There wild woods grow, and rivers row
    And monie a hill between,
But day and night my fancy's flight
    Is ever wi my Jean.

I see her in the dewy flowers –
    I see her sweet and fair.
I hear her in the tunefu birds –
    I hear her charm the air.
There's not a bonie flower that springs
    By fountain, shaw or green,
There's not a bonie bird that sings,
    But minds me o my Jean.

Jumpin John

Chorus
The lang lad they ca' Jumpin John
    Beguil'd the bonie lassie!
The lang lad they ca' Jumpin John
    Beguil'd the bonie lassie!

Her daddie forbad, her minnie forbad;
    Forbidden she wadna be:
She wadna trow't, the browst she brew'd
    Wad taste sae bitterlie!

A cow and a cauf, a yowe and a hauf,
    And thretty guid shillins and three:
A vera guid tocher, a cotter-man's dochter,
    The lass with the bonie black e'e.

Up in the Morning Early

Chorus
Up in the morning's no for me,
*   Up in the morning early!*
When a' the hills are cover'd wi snaw
*   I'm sure it's winter fairly!*

Cauld blaws the wind frae east to west,
    The drift is driving sairly,
Sae loud and shrill's I hear the blast –
    I'm sure it's winter fairly!

The birds sit chittering in the thorn,
    A day they fare but sparely;
And lang's the night frae e'en to morn –
    I'm sure it's winter fairly!

On Scaring some Water-fowl
in Loch Turit

Why, ye tenants of the lake,
For me your wat'ry haunt forsake?
Tell me, fellow-creatures, why
At my presence thus you fly?
Why disturb your social joys,
Parent, filial, kindred ties? –
Common friend to you and me,
Nature's gifts to all are free:
Peaceful keep your dimpling wave,
Busy feed, or wanton lave;
Or, beneath the sheltering rock,
Bide the surging billow's shock.

    Conscious, blushing for our race,
Soon, too soon, your fears I trace.
Man, your proud, usurping foe,
Would be lord of all below:
Plumes himself in freedom's pride,
Tyrant stern to all beside.

The eagle, from the cliffy brow,
Marking you his prey below,
In his breast no pity dwells,
Strong necessity compels:
But Man, to whom alone is giv'n
A ray direct from pitying Heav'n,
Glories in his heart humane –
And creatures for his pleasure slain!

In these savage, liquid plains,
Only known to wand'ring swains,
Where the mossy riv'let strays
Far from human haunts and ways,
All on Nature you depend,
And life's poor season peaceful spend.

Or, if Man's superior might
Dare invade your native right,
On the lofty ether borne,
Man with all his powers you scorn;
Swiftly seek, on clanging wings,
Other lakes, and other springs;
And the foe you cannot brave,
Scorn at least to be his slave.

From Epistle to Davie, a Brother Poet

What tho, like commoners of air,
We wander out, we know not where,
    But either house or hal'?
Yet Nature's charms, the hills and woods,
The sweeping vales, and foaming floods,
    Are free alike to all.
In days when daisies deck the ground,
    And blackbirds whistle clear,
With honest joy our hearts will bound,
    To see the coming year:
        On braes when we please then,
            We'll sit and sowth a tune;
        Syne rhyme till't, we'll time till't,
            An sing't when we hae done.

As I Stood by Yon Roofless Tower

Chorus
A lassie all alone, was making her moan
Lamenting our lads beyond the sea:-
'In the bluidy wars they fa', and our honor's gane an a',
And broken-hearted we maun die.'

As I stood by yon roofless tower,
Where the wa'flow'r scents the dewy air,
Where the houlet mourns in her ivy bower,
And tells the midnight moon her care:

The winds were laid, the air was still,
The stars they shot along the sky,
The tod was howling on the hill,
And the distant-echoing glens reply.

The burn, adown its hazelly path,
Was rushing by the ruin'd wa',
Hasting to join the sweeping Nith,
Whase roaring seemed to rise and fa'.

The cauld blae North was streaming forth
Her lights, wi hissing, eerie din:
Athort the lift they start and shift,
Like Fortune's favors, tint as win.

Now, looking over firth and fauld,
    Her horn the pale-faced Cynthia rear'd.
When lo! in form of minstrel auld
    A stern and stalwart ghaist appear'd.

And frae his harp sic strains did flow,
    Might rous'd the slumbering Dead to hear,
But O, it was a tale of woe
    As ever met a Briton's ear!

He sang wi joy his former day,
    He, weeping, wail'd his latter times:
But what he said – it was nae play!
    I winna ventur't in my rhymes.

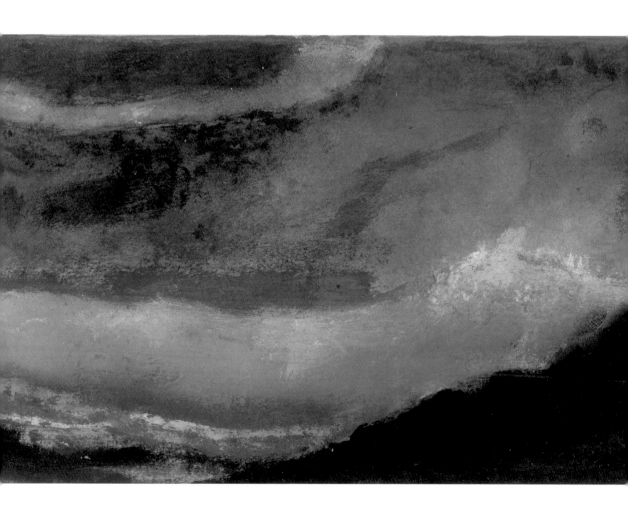

Phillis the Fair

While larks, with little wing, fann'd the pure air,
Viewing the breathing Spring, forth I did fare.
  Gay, the sun's golden eye
  Peep'd o'er the mountains high;
'Such thy bloom,' did I cry, 'Phillis the fair!'

In each bird's careless song, glad, I did share;
While yon wild flowers among, chance led me there.
  Sweet to the opening day,
  Rosebuds bent the dewy spray;
'Such thy bloom,' did I say – 'Phillis the fair!'

Down in the shady walk, doves cooing were;
I mark'd the cruel hawk caught in a snare.
  So kind may Fortune be!
  Such make his destiny,
He who would injure thee, Phillis the fair!

Willie Wastle

Willie Wastle dwalt on Tweed,
    The spot they ca'd it Linkumdoddie.
Willie was a wabster guid
    Could stown a clue wi onie body.
He had a wife was dour and din,
    O, Tinkler Maidgie was her mither!
Sic a wife as Willie had,
    I would na gie a button for her.

She has an e'e (she has but ane),
    The cat has twa the very colour,
Five rusty teeth, forbye a stump,
    A clapper-tongue wad deave a miller;
A whiskin beard about her mou,
    Her nose and chin they threaten ither;
Sic a wife as Willie had,
    I wad na gie a button for her.

She's bow-hough'd, she's hem-shin'd,
    Ae limpin leg a hand-breed shorter;
She's twisted right, she's twisted left,
    To balance fair in ilka quarter;
She has a hump upon her breast,
    The twin o that upon her shouther:
Sic a wife as Willie had,
    I wad na gie a button for her.

Auld baudrans by the ingle sits,
    An wi her loof her face a-washin;
But Willie's wife is nae sae trig,
    She dights her grunzie wi a hushion;
Her walie nieves like midden-creels,
    Her face wad fyle the Logan Water;
Sic a wife as Willie had,
    I wad na gie a button for her.

I do Confess Thou art sae Fair

I do confess thou art sae fair,
    I wad been o'er the lugs in luve,
Had I na found the slightest prayer
    That lips could speak thy heart could muve.

I do confess thee sweet, but find
    Thou art so thriftless o thy sweets,
Thy favours are the silly wind
    That kisses ilka thing it meets.

See yonder rosebud rich in dew,
    Amang its native briers sae coy,
How sune it tines its scent and hue,
    When pu'd and worn a common toy!

Sic fate ere lang shall thee betide,
    Tho thou may gaily bloom awhile,
And sune thou shalt be thrown aside,
    Like onie common weed, an vile.

Galloway Tam

O Galloway Tam came here to woo,
    I'd rather we'd gin him the brawnit cow;
For our lass Bess may curse and ban
    The wanton wit o Galloway Tam.

O Galloway Tam came here to shear,
    I'd rather we'd gin him the gude gray mare;
He kist the gudewife and strack the gudeman,
    And that's the tricks o Galloway Tam.

From **Epistle to John Rankine**

It pits me ay as mad's a hare;
So I can rhyme nor write nae mair;
But pennyworths again is fair,
    When time's expedient:
Meanwhile, I am, respected Sir,
    Your most obedient.

My Luve is like A Red, Red Rose

O, my luve is like a red, red rose,
    That's newly sprung in June.
O, my luve is like the melodie,
    That's sweetly play'd in tune.

As fair art thou, my bonie lass,
    So deep in luve am I,
And I will luve thee still, my dear,
    Till a' the seas gang dry.

Till a' the seas gang dry, my dear,
    And the rocks melt wi the sun!
And I will luve thee still, my dear,
    While the sands o life shall run.

And fare thee weel, my only luve,
    And fare thee weel, a while!
And I will come again, my luve,
    Tho it were ten thousand mile!

RED
ROSE

From **The Twa Herds**

What herd like Russell tell'd his tale?
His voice was heard thro muir and dale;
He ken'd the Lord's sheep, ilka tail,
    O'er a' the height;
And tell'd gin they were sick or hale,
    At the first sight.

From **Despondency, an Ode**

Ye tiny elves that guiltless sport,
    Like linnets in the bush,
Ye little know the ills ye court,
    When manhood is your wish!
        The losses, the crosses,
            That active man enrage;
        The fears all, the tears all,
            Of dim declining Age!

From **The Brigs of Ayr**

Nae mair the flower in field or meadow springs;
Nae mair the grove with airy concert rings,
Except perhaps the robin's whistling glee,
Proud o the height o some bit half-lang tree;
The hoary morns precede the sunny days,
Mild, calm, serene, widespreads the noontide blaze,
While thick the gossamour waves wanton in the rays.

From **The Posie**

The woodbine I will pu, when the e'ening star is near,
And the diamond draps o dew shall be her een sae clear!
The violet's for modesty, which weel she fa's to wear –
    And a' to be a posie to my ain dear May!

From **Adown Winding Nith**

The Daisy amus'd my fond fancy,
 So artless, so simple, so wild:
'Thou emblem,' said I, 'o my Phyllis' –
 For she is Simplicity's child.

The rosebud's the blush o my charmer,
 Her sweet balmy lip when 'tis prest.
How fair and how pure is the lily!
 But fairer and purer her breast.

Yon knot of gay flowers in the arbour,
 They ne'er wi my Phillis can vie;
Her breath is the breath o the woodbine,
 Its dew-drop o diamond her eye.

Now Spring has clad the Grove in Green

Now Spring has clad the grove in green,
    And strew'd the lea wi flowers;
The furrow'd, waving corn is seen
    Rejoice in fostering showers;
While ilka thing in nature join
    Their sorrows to forego,
O, why thus all alone are mine
    The weary steps o woe!

The trout within yon wimpling burn
    Glides swift, a silver dart,
And, safe beneath the shady thorn,
    Defies the angler's art:
My life was ance that careless stream
    That wanton trout was I.
But Love wi unrelenting beam
    Has scorch'd my fountains dry.

The waken'd lav'rock warbling springs,
    And climbs the early sky,
Winnowing blythe his dewy wings
    In Morning's rosy eye:
As little reck't I Sorrow's power,
    Until the flowery snare
O witching Love, in luckless hour,
    Made me the thrall o care!

From **O, were my Love**

O, were my love yon lilac fair
Wi purple blossoms to the spring
And I a bird to shelter there,
When wearied on my little wing.

Epitaph on a Henpecked Squire

As father Adam first was fool'd,
    A case that's still too common,
Here lies a man a woman ruled -
    The Devil ruled the woman.

From The Twa Dogs

The first I'll name, they ca'd him Caesar,
Was keepit for 'his Honor's' pleasure:
His hair, his size, his mouth, his lugs,
Shew'd he was nane o Scotland's dogs;
But whalpit some place far abroad,
Whare sailors gang to fish for cod.

The tither was a ploughman's collie,
A rhyming, ranting, raving billie,
Wha for his friend an comrade had him,
And in his freaks had Luath ca'd him,
After some dog in Highland sang,
Was made lang syne - Lord knows how lang.

He was a gash an faithfu tyke,
As ever lap a sheugh or dyke.
His honest, sonsie, baws'nt face
Ay gat him friends in ilka place;
His breast was white, his tousie back
Weel clad wi coat o glossy black;
His gawsie tail, wi upward curl,
Hung owre his hurdies wi a swirl.

From **The Brigs of Ayr**

'Twas when the stacks get on their winter hap,
And thack and rape secure the toil-won crap;
Potatoe-bings are snuggèd up frae skaith
O coming Winter's biting, frosty breath;
The bees, rejoicing o'er their summer toils -
Unnumber'd buds' an flowers' delicious spoils,
Sealed up with frugal care in massive waxen piles.

The Night was Still

The night was still, and o'er the hill
    The moon shone on the castle wa',
The mavis sang, while dew-drops hang
    Around her on the castle wa':

Sae merrily they danc'd the ring
    Frae eenin till the cocks did craw,
And ay the o'erword o the spring
    Was: - 'Irvine's bairns are bonie a'!'

From Highland Mary

Ye banks and braes and streams around
    The castle o Montgomery,
Green be your woods, and fair your flowers,
    Your waters never drumlie!
There Summer first unfald her robes,
    And there the longest tarry!
And there I took the last fareweel
    O my sweet Highland Mary!

How sweetly bloom'd the gay, green birk,
    How rich the hawthorn's blossom,
As underneath their fragrant shade
    I clasp'd her to my bosom!
The golden hours on angel wings
    Flew o'er me and my dearie:
For dear to me as light and life
    Was my sweet Highland Mary.

From **Tam Lin**

About the middle o the night
    She heard the bridles ring;
This lady was as glad at that
    As any earthly thing.

First she let the black pass by,
    And syne she let the brown;
But quickly she ran to the milk-white steed,
    And pu'd the rider down.

As I cam o'er the Cairney Mount

Oh my bonie Highland lad,
    My winsome, weelfar'd Highland laddie;
Wha wad mind the wind and rain,
    Sae weel row'd in his tartan plaidie.

 As I cam o'er the Cairney mount,
    And down amang the blooming heather,
Kindly stood the milkin-shiel
    To shelter frae the stormy weather.

Now Phebus blinkit on the bent,
    And o'er the knowes the lambs were bleating:
But he wan my heart's consent,
    To be his ain at the neist meeting.

Bonie Peg-a-Ramsay

Cauld is the e'enin blast
    O Boreas o'er the pool
And dawin, it is dreary,
    When birks are bare at Yule.

O, cauld blaws the e'enin blast
    When bitter bites the frost,
And in the mirk and dreary drift
    The hills and glens are lost!

Ne'er sae murky blew the night
    That drifted o'er the hill,
But bonie Peg-a-Ramsay
    Gat grist to her mill.

The Auld Farmer's New-Year
Morning Salutation to his Auld Mare, Maggie
On giving her the accustomed ripp of corn to hansel in the New-Year

A Guid New-Year I wish thee, Maggie!
Hae, there's a ripp to thy auld baggie:
Tho thou's howe-backit now, an knaggie,
    I've seen the day
Thou could hae gaen like onie staggie,
    Out-owre the lay.

Tho now thou's dowie, stiff an crazy,
An thy auld hide as white's a daisie,
I've seen thee dappl't, sleek an glaizie,
    A bonie gray:
He should been tight that daur't to raize thee,
    Ance in a day.

Thou ance was i' the foremost rank,
A filly buirdly, steeve an swank:
An set weel down a shapely shank,
    As e'er tread yird;
An could hae flown out-owre a stank,
    Like onie bird.

It's now some nine-an-twenty year
Sin' thou was my guid-father's meere;
He gied me thee, o tocher clear,
    An fifty mark;
Tho it was sma', 'twas weel-won gear,
    An thou was stark.

From **Now Westlin Winds**

Now westlin winds and slaught'ring guns
    Bring Autumn's pleasant weather;
The moorcock springs on whirring wings
    Amang the blooming heather:
Now waving grain, wide o'er the plain,
    Delights the weary farmer;
The moon shines bright, as I rove by night,
    To muse upon my charmer.

The paitrick lo'es the fruitfu fells,
    The plover lo'es the mountains;
The woodcock haunts the lonely dells;
    The soaring hern the fountains:
Thro lofty groves the cushat roves,
    The path o man to shun it;
The hazel bush o'erhangs the thrush,
    The spreading thorn the linnet.

From **A Winter Night**

When biting Boreas, fell and doure,
Sharp shivers thro the leafless bow'r;
When Phoebus gies a short-liv'd glow'r,
    Far south the lift,
Dim-dark'ning thro the flaky show'r,
    Or whirling drift:

Ae night the storm the steeples rocked;
Poor Labour sweet in sleep was locked;
While burns, wi snawy wreaths up-choked,
    Wild-eddying swirl;
Or thro the mining outlet bocked,
    Down headlong hurl:

List'ning the doors an winnocks rattle,
I thought me on the ourie cattle,
Or silly sheep, wha bide this brattle
    O winter war,
And thro the drift, deep-lairing, sprattle
    Beneath a scaur.

And Maun I Still on Menie Doat

Chorus
And maun I still on Menie doat,
*   And bear the scorn that's in her e'e?*
For it's jet, jet-black, an it's like a hawk,
*   An it winna let a body be.*

Again rejoicing Nature sees
    Her robe assume its vernal hues:
Her leafy locks wave in the breeze,
    All freshly steep'd in morning dews.

In vain to me the cowslips blaw,
    In vain to me the vi'lets spring;
In vain to me in glen or shaw,
    The mavis and the lint-white sing.

The merry ploughboy cheers his team
    Wi joy the tentie seedsman stalks;
But life's to me a weary dream,
    A dream of ane that never wauks.

The wanton coot the water skims,
    Amang the reeds the ducklings cry,
The stately swan majestic swims,
    And ev'ry thing is blest but I.

The sheep-herd steeks his faulding slap,
　　And o'er the moorlands whistles shrill;
Wi wild, unequal, wand'ring step,
　　I meet him on the dewy hill.

And when the lark, 'tween light and dark,
　　Blythe waukens by the daisy's side,
And mounts and sings on flittering wings,
　　A woe-worn ghaist I hameward glide.

Come winter, with thine angry howl,
　　And raging, bend the naked tree;
Thy gloom will soothe my cheerless soul,
　　When nature all is sad like me!

Amang the Trees

Amang the trees, where humming bees
    At buds and flowers were hinging, O,
Auld Caledon drew out her drone,
    And to her pipe was singing, O.
'Twas Pibroch, Sang, Strathspeys and Reels -
    She dirl'd them aff fu clearly, O,
When there cam a yell o foreign squeels,
    That dang her tapsalteerie, O!

Their capon craws and queer 'ha ha's',
    They made our lugs grow eerie, O.
The hungry bike did scrape and fyke,
    Till we were wae and weary, O.
But a royal ghaist, wha ance was cas'd
    A prisoner, aughteen year awa,
He fir'd a Fiddler in the North,
    That dang them tapsalteerie, O!

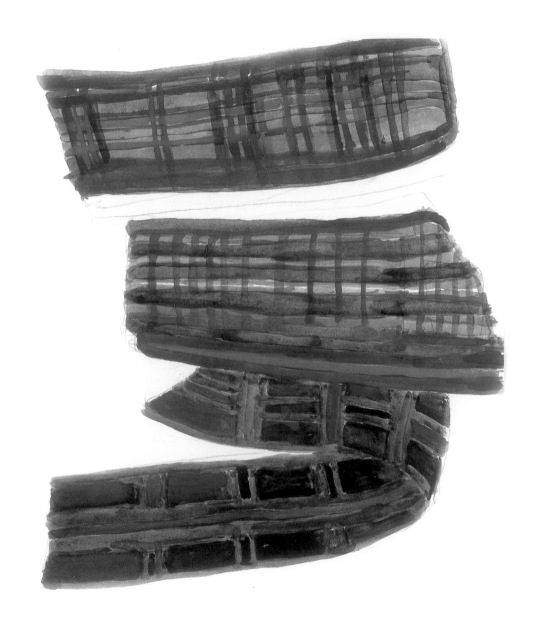

Lines on the Falls of Fyers
Near Loch Ness Written with a pencil on the spot

Among the heathy hills and ragged woods
The roaring Fyers pours his mossy floods;
Till full he dashes on the rocky mounds,
Where, thro a shapeless breach, his stream resounds,
As high in air the bursting torrents flow,
As deep recoiling surges foam below,
Prone down the rock the whitening sheet descends,
And viewless Echo's ear, astonish'd, rends.
Dim-seen, through rising mists and ceaseless show'rs
The hoary cavern, wide-surrounding, lours:
Still thro the gap the struggling river toils,
And still, below, the horrid caldron boils -

A Sonnet upon Sonnets

Fourteen, a sonneteer thy praises sings;
What magic myst'ries in that number lie!
Your hen hath fourteen eggs beneath her wings
That fourteen chickens to the roost may fly.
Fourteen full pounds the jockey's stone must be;
His age fourteen – a horse's prime is past.
Fourteen long hours too oft the Bard must fast;
Fourteen bright bumpers – bliss he ne'er must see!
Before fourteen, a dozen yields the strife;
Before fourteen – e'en thirteen's strength is vain.
Fourteen good years – a woman gives us life;
Fourteen good men – we lose that life again.
What lucubrations can be more upon it?
Fourteen good measur'd verses make a sonnet.

Bessy and her Spinnin-Wheel

O, leeze me on my spinnin-wheel!
And leeze me on my rock and reel,
Frae tap to tae that cleeds me bien,
And haps me fiel and warm at e'en!
I'll set me down, and sing and spin,
While laigh descends the summer sun,
Blest wi content, and milk and meal –
O, leeze me on my spinnin-wheel!

On ilka hand the burnies trot,
And meet below my theekit cot.
The scented birk and hawthorn white
Across the pool their arms unite,
Alike to screen the birdie's nest
And little fishes' caller rest.
The sun blinks kindly in the biel,
Where blythe I turn my spinnin-wheel.

On lofty aiks the cushats wail,
And Echo cons the doolfu tale.
The lintwhites in the hazel braes,
Delighted, rival ither's lays.
The craik amang the claver hay,
The paitrick whirrin o'er the ley,
The swallow jinkin round my shiel,
Amuse me at my spinnin-wheel.

Wi sma' to sell and less to buy,
Aboon distress, below envy,
O, wha wad leave this humble state
For a' the pride of a' the great?
Amid their flaring, idle toys,
Amid their cumbrous, dinsome joys,
Can they the peace and pleasure feel
Of Bessy at her spinnin-wheel?

On Chloris

Requesting me to give her a sprig of blossomed thorn

From the white-blossom'd sloe my dear Chloris requested
    A sprig, her fair breast to adorn:
No, by Heaven! I exclaim'd 'let me perish for ever
    Ere I plant in that bosom a thorn!'

Address to the Shade of Thomson

On crowning his bust at Ednam, Roxburghshire, with a Wreath of bays

While virgin Spring by Eden's flood
    Unfolds her tender mantle green,
Or pranks the sod in frolic mood,
    Or tunes Eolian strains between.

While Summer with a matron grace,
    Retreats to Dryburgh's cooling shade,
Yet oft, delighted, stops to trace
    The progress of the spikey blade:

While Autumn, benefactor kind,
    By Tweed erects his aged head,
And sees, with self-approving mind,
    Each creature on his bounty fed.

While maniac Winter rages o'er
    The hills whence classic Yarrow flows,
Rousing the turbid torrent's roar,
    Or sweeping, wild, a waste of snows.

So long, sweet Poet of the year!
    Shall bloom that wreath thou well hast won;
While Scotia, with exulting tear,
    Proclaims that Thomson is her son.

The Bonie Moor-Hen

Chorus
I rede you, beware at the hunting, young men!
I rede you, beware at the hunting, young men!
Take some on the wing, and some as they spring,
But cannily steal on a bonie moor-hen.

The heather was blooming, the meadows were mawn,
Our lads gaed a-hunting ae day at the dawn,
O'er moors and o'er mosses and monie a glen:
At length they discovered a bonie moor-hen.

Sweet-brushing the dew from the brown heather bells,
Her colours betray'd her on yon mossy fells!
Her plumage outlustred the pride o the spring,
And O as she wanton'd sae gay on the wing.

Auld Phoebus himsel, as he peep'd o'er the hill,
In spite at her plumage he tryed his skill:
He levell'd his rays where she bask'd on the brae –
His rays were outshone, and but mark'd where she lay!

They hunted the valley, they hunted the hill,
The best of our lads wi the best o their skill;
But still as the fairest she sat in their sight.
Then whirr! she was over, a mile at a flight.

To Miss Isabella Macleod

Edinburgh, March 16, 1787

The crimson blossom charms the bee,
    The summer sun the swallow:
So dear this tuneful gift to me
    From lovely Isabella.

Her portrait fair upon my mind
    Revolving time shall mellow,
And mem'ry's latest efforts find
    The lovely Isabella.

No Bard nor lover's rapture this
    In fancies vain and shallow!
She is, so come my soul to bliss,
    The lovely Isabella.

My Bonie Bell

The smiling Spring comes in rejoicing,
    And surly Winter grimly flies.
Now crystal clear are the falling waters,
    And bonie blue are the sunny skies.
Fresh o'er the mountains breaks forth the morning,
    The ev'ning gilds the ocean's swell:
All creatures joy in the sun's returning,
    And I rejoice in my bonie Bell.

The flowery Spring leads sunny Summer,
    The yellow Autumn presses near;
Then in his turn comes gloomy Winter,
    Till smiling Spring again appear.
Thus seasons dancing, life advancing,
    Old Time and Nature their changes tell;
But never ranging, still unchanging,
    I adore my bonie Bell.

The Gallant Weaver

Where Cart rins rowin to the sea
By monie a flower and spreading tree,
There lives a lad, the lad for me –
    He is a gallant weaver!
O, I had wooers aught or nine,
They gied me rings and ribbons fine,
And I was fear'd my heart wad tine,
    And I gied it to the weaver.

My daddie sign'd my tocher-band
To gie the lad that has the land,
But to my heart I'll add my hand
    And give it to the weaver.
While birds rejoice in leafy bowers,
While bees delight in opening flowers,
While corn grows green in summer showers,
    I love my gallant weaver.

Inscription at Friars' Carse Hermitage

To the Memory of Robert Riddell

To Riddell, much lamented man,
    This ivied cot was dear:
Wand'rer, dost value matchless worth?
    This ivied cot revere.

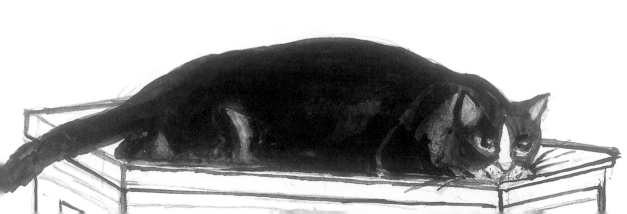

Banks of Cree
(Here is the Glen)

Here is the glen, and here the bower
    All underneath the birchen shade,
The village-bell has toll'd the hour –
    O, what can stay my lovely maid?

'Tis not Maria's whispering call –
    'Tis but the balmy-breathing gale,
Mixed with some warbler's dying fall
    The dewy star of eve to hail!

It is Maria's voice I hear –
    So calls the woodlark in the grove
His little faithful mate to cheer:
    At once 'tis music and 'tis love!

And art thou come? And art thou true?
    O, welcome, dear, to love and me,
And let us all our vows renew
    Along the flowery banks of Cree!

From **Dumfries Epigrams**

Baillie Swan, Baillie Swan,
Let you do what you can,
God ha' mercy on honest Dumfries:
But e'er the year's done,
Good Lord! Provost John
Will find that his Swans are but Geese.

To the Woodlark

O, stay, sweet warbling wood-lark, stay,
Nor quit for me the trembling spray!
A hapless lover courts thy lay,
    Thy soothing, fond complaining.
Again, again that tender part,
That I may catch thy melting art!
For surely that wad touch her heart,
    Wha kills me wi disdaining.

Say, was thy little mate unkind,
And heard thee as the careless wind?
O, nocht but love and sorrow join'd
    Sic notes o woe could wauken!
Thou tells o never-ending care,
O speechless grief and dark despair –
For pity's sake, sweet bird, nae mair,
    Or my poor heart is broken!

Their Groves o Sweet Myrtle

A tribute to Jean Armour, April 1795

Their groves o sweet myrtle let foreign lands reckon,
    Where bright-beaming summers exalt the perfume!
Far dearer to me yon lone glen o green breckan,
    Wi the burn stealing under the lang, yellow broom;
Far dearer to me are yon humble broom bowers,
    Where the blue-bell and gowan lurk lowly, unseen;
For there, lightly tripping among the wild flowers,
    A-list'ning the linnet, aft wanders my Jean.

Tho rich is the breeze in their gay, sunny vallies,
    And cauld Caledonia's blast on the wave,
Their sweet-scented woodlands that skirt the proud palace,
    What are they? – The haunt of the tyrant and slave!
The slave's spicy forests and gold-bubbling fountains
    The brave Caledonian views wi disdain:
He wanders as free as the winds of his mountains,
    Save Love's willing fetters – the chains o his Jean.

The Wren's Nest

The Robin cam to the wren's nest
    And keekit in and keekit in,
O weel's me on your auld pow,
    Wad ye be in, wad ye be in.
Ye'se ne'er get leave to lie without,
    And I within, and I within,
As lang's I hae an auld clout
    To row you in, to row you in.

Raging Fortune

O, raging Fortune's withering blast
    Has laid my leaf full low!
O, raging Fortune's withering blast
    Has laid my leaf full low!

My stem was fair, my bud was green,
    My blossom sweet did blow;
The dew fell fresh, the sun rose mild,
    And made my branches grow.

But luckless Fortune's northern storms
    Laid a' my blossoms low!
But luckless Fortune's northern storms
    Laid a' my blossoms low!

Dainty Davie

Meet me on the Warlock Knowe,
*   Dainty Davie, Dainty Davie!*
There I'll spend the day wi you,
*   My ain dear Dainty Davie.*

Now rosy May comes in wi flowers
To deck her gay, green-spreading bowers;
And now comes in the happy hours
    To wander wi my Davie.

The crystal waters round us fa'
The merry birds are lovers a',
The scented breezes round us blaw
    A wandering wi my Davie.

When purple morning starts the hare
To steal upon her early fare,
Then thro the dews I will repair
    To meet my faithfu Davie.

When day, expiring in the west,
The curtain draws o Nature's rest,
I flee to his arms I loe the best:
    And that's my ain dear Davie!

Reply to an invitation

Sir,

Yours this moment I unseal,
　　And faith! I'm gay and hearty.
To tell the truth and shame the Deil,
　　I am as fou as Bartie.
But Foorsday, Sir, my promise leal,
　　Expect me o your partie,
If on a beastie I can speel
　　Or hurl in a cartie.
Yours,
ROBERT BURNS